A CENTURY of
BIRKENHEAD
and WIRRAL

Birkenhead Town Hall really dominates Hamilton Square, seen here in the early 1930s.

A CENTURY of BIRKENHEAD and WIRRAL

CLIFF HAYES

First published in 2000 by Sutton Publishing

This new paperback edition first published in 2007 by Sutton Publishing

Reprinted in 2008 by
The History Press
The Mill, Brimscombe Port,
Stroud, Gloucestershire, GL5 2QG
www.thehistorypress.co.uk

Reprinted 2010, 2011, 2012

British Library Cataloguing in Publication Data
A catalogue record for this book is available from the British Library.

ISBN 978-0-7509-4904-0

Front endpaper: Westbourne Road, New Brighton, *c.* 1905.
Back endpaper: New Brighton funfair, mid-1950s. (*Len Jackson*)
Half title page: Composite Birkenhead postcard by Valentine's from 1938.
Title page: Day trippers take a rest at New Brighton funfair, Easter 1959. (*Keith Medley*)

> *Dedicated to*
> *Olive Corson of Ellesmere Port who on*
> *19 November 1945 had a son she called John*

A derelict ship on the shore at Hoylake in 1934. (*Philip A. Cox*)

Typeset in 11/14pt Photina.
Typesetting and origination by
Sutton Publishing Limited.
Printed and bound in England.

Contents

Foreword

BY THE WORSHIPFUL THE MAYOR OF WIRRAL
COUNCILLOR MRS KATE WOOD

As the Mayor of Wirral, an office I hold with great pride, it is a privilege to write this foreword, about the last hundred years of the life and history of this very splendid peninsula.

Wirral is an area of great contrasts and great people, who are consumed with pride in the place and take a very serious interest in all that happens here. Apart from those who were born here, the population also has many residents who have settled from Liverpool, Ireland, Wales, Scotland and further afield. Thus life is interesting.

Many of our older people experienced austerity and the hardship of war. Indeed many fought for their country. We are proud of them and grateful for the years of peace we have enjoyed.

Wirral has a great history of ship building. Everyone was devastated by the demise of Cammell Laird's in the 1980s although, thankfully, some of the yard came back into business for ship repairs in the 1990s.

Since Wirral Borough Council came into being in 1974, there has been much regeneration in the older parts of Birkenhead and Wallasey and the development of tourism and small businesses which benefit the local economy and jobs.

Set between the Mersey and the Dee we have green belt, beaches, sailing and many golf courses. Wirral is indeed a leisure peninsula, with a strong maritime background. The last hundred years has brought many changes, well documented in this book. We all look forward to, and are prepared for, an exciting new century.

Please enjoy this book.

Mayor of Wirral
Mayor's Parlour
Town Hall
Wallasey
Wirral, CH44 8ED

HM Submarine *Revenge* about to be launched into the River Mersey from Cammell Laird's shipyard, 1967.

Britain: A Century of Change

Two women encumbered with gas masks go about their daily tasks during the early days of the war. (*Hulton Getty Picture Collection*)

The sixty years ending in 1900 were a period of huge trans-formation for Britain. Railway stations, post-and-telegraph offices, police and fire stations, gasworks and gasometers, new livestock markets and covered markets, schools, churches, football grounds, hospitals and asylums, water pumping stations and sewerage plants totally altered the urban scene, and the country's population tripled with more than seven out of ten people being born in or moving to the towns. The century that followed, leading up to the Millennium's end in 2000, was to be a period of even greater change.

When Queen Victoria died in 1901, she was measured for her coffin by her grandson Kaiser Wilhelm, the London prostitutes put on black mourning and the blinds came down in the villas and terraces spreading out from the old town centres. These centres were reachable by train and tram, by the new bicycles and still newer motor cars, were connected by the new telephone, and lit by gas or even electricity. The shops may have been full of British-made cotton and woollen clothing but the grocers and butchers were selling cheap Danish bacon, Argentinian beef, Australasian mutton and tinned or dried fish and fruit from Canada, California and South Africa. Most of these goods were carried in British-built-and-crewed ships burning Welsh steam coal.

As the first decade moved on, the Open Spaces Act meant more parks, bowling greens and cricket pitches. The First World War transformed the place of women, as they took over many men's jobs. Its other legacies were the war memorials which joined the statues of Victorian worthies in main squares round the land. After 1918 death duties and higher taxation bit hard, and a quarter of England changed hands in the space of only a few years.

The multiple shop – the chain store – appeared in the high street: Sainsburys, Maypole, Lipton's, Home & Colonial, the Fifty Shilling Tailor, Burton, Boots, W.H. Smith. The shopper was spoilt for choice, attracted by the brash fascias and advertising hoardings for national brands like Bovril, Pears Soap, and Ovaltine. Many new buildings began to be seen, such as garages, motor showrooms, picture palaces (cinemas), 'palais de dance', and ribbons of 'semis' stretched along the roads and new bypasses and onto the new estates nudging the green belts.

During the 1920s cars became more reliable and sophisticated as well as commonplace, with developments like the electric self-starter making them easier for women to drive. Who wanted to turn a crank handle in the new short skirt? This was, indeed, the electric age as much as the motor era. Trolley buses, electric trams and trains extended mass transport and electric light replaced gas in the street and the home, which itself was groomed by the vacuum cleaner.

A major jolt to the march onward and upward was administered by the Great Depression of the early 1930s. The older British industries

– textiles, shipbuilding, iron, steel, coal – were already under pressure from foreign competition when this worldwide slump arrived. Luckily there were new diversions to alleviate the misery. The 'talkies' arrived in the cinemas; more and more radios and gramophones were to be found in people's homes; there were new women's magazines, with fashion, cookery tips and problem pages; football pools; the flying feats of women pilots like Amy Johnson; the Loch Ness Monster; cheap chocolate and the drama of Edward VIII's abdication.

Things were looking up again by 1936 and new light industry was booming in the Home Counties as factories struggled to keep up with the demand for radios, radiograms, cars and electronic goods, including the first television sets. The threat from Hitler's Germany meant rearmament, particularly of the airforce, which stimulated aircraft and aero engine firms. If you were lucky and lived in the south, there was good money to be earned. A semi-detached house cost £450, a Morris Cowley £150. People may have smoked like chimneys but life expectancy, since 1918, was up by 15 years while the birth rate had almost halved.

In some ways it is the little memories that seem to linger longest from the Second World War: the kerbs painted white to show up in the

A W.H.Smith shop front in Beaconsfield, 1922.

blackout, the rattle of ack-ack shrap-
nel on roof tiles, sparrows killed by
bomb blast. The biggest damage, apart
from London, was in the south-west
(Plymouth, Bristol) and the Midlands
(Coventry, Birmingham). Postwar
reconstruction was rooted in the
Beveridge Report which set out the
expectations for the Welfare State.
This, together with the nationalisation
of the Bank of England, coal, gas,
electricity and the railways, formed the
programme of the Labour government
in 1945.

Times were hard in the late 1940s,
with rationing even more stringent
than during the war. Yet this was, as

Children collecting
aluminium to help the
war effort, London,
1940s. (*IWM*)

has been said, 'an innocent and well-behaved era'. The first let-up came
in 1951 with the Festival of Britain and there was another fillip in 1953
from the Coronation, which incidentally gave a huge boost to the spread
of TV. By 1954 leisure motoring had been resumed but the Comet –
Britain's best hope for taking on the American aviation industry – suffered
a series of mysterious crashes. The Suez debacle of 1956 was followed
by an acceleration in the withdrawal from Empire, which had begun in
1947 with the Independence of India. Consumerism was truly born with
the advent of commercial TV and most homes soon boasted washing
machines, fridges, electric irons and fires.

A street party to
celebrate the Queen's
Coronation, June
1953. (*Hulton Getty
Picture Collection*)

The *Lady Chatterley* obscenity trial in 1960
was something of a straw in the wind for
what was to follow in that decade. A collective
loss of inhibition seemed to sweep the land, as
the Beatles and the Rolling Stones transformed
popular music, and retailing, cinema and the
theatre were revolutionised. Designers, hair-
dressers, photographers and models moved
into places vacated by an Establishment put
to flight by the new breed of satirists spawned
by *Beyond the Fringe* and *Private Eye*.

In the 1970s Britain seems to have
suffered a prolonged hangover after the
excesses of the previous decade. Ulster,
inflation and union troubles were not made
up for by entry into the EEC, North Sea Oil,
Women's Lib or, indeed, Punk Rock. Mrs

Thatcher applied the corrective in the 1980s, as the country moved more and more from its old manufacturing base over to providing services, consulting, advertising, and expertise in the 'invisible' market of high finance or in IT.

The post-1945 townscape has seen changes to match those in the worlds of work, entertainment and politics. In 1952 the Clean Air Act served notice on smogs and pea-souper fogs, smuts and blackened buildings, forcing people to stop burning coal and go over to smokeless sources of heat and energy. In the same decade some of the best urban building took place in the 'new towns' like Basildon, Crawley, Stevenage and Harlow. Elsewhere open warfare was declared on slums and what was labelled inadequate, cramped, back-to-back, two-up, two-down, housing. The new 'machine for living in' was a flat in a high-rise block. The architects and planners who promoted these were in league with the traffic engineers, determined to keep the motor car moving whatever the price in multi-storey car parks, meters, traffic wardens and ring roads. The old pollutant, coal smoke, was replaced by petrol and diesel exhaust, and traffic noise.

Fast food was no longer only a pork pie in a pub or fish-and-chips. There were Indian curry houses, Chinese take-aways and American-style hamburgers, while the drinker could get away from beer in a wine bar. Under the impact of television the big Gaumonts and Odeons closed or were rebuilt as multi-screen cinemas, while the palais de dance gave way to discos and clubs.

Punk rockers demonstrate their anarchic style during the 1970s. (*Barnaby's Picture Library*)

From the late 1960s the introduction of listed buildings and conservation areas, together with the growth of preservation societies, put a brake on 'comprehensive redevelopment'. The end of the century and the start of the Third Millennium see new challenges to the health of towns and the wellbeing of the nine out of ten people who now live urban lives. The fight is on to prevent town centres from dying, as patterns of housing and shopping change, and edge-of-town supermarkets exercise the attractions of one-stop shopping. But as banks and department stores close, following the haberdashers, greengrocers, butchers and ironmongers, there are signs of new growth such as farmers' markets, and corner stores acting as pick-up points where customers collect shopping ordered on-line from web sites.

Millennium celebrations over the Thames at Westminster, New Year's Eve, 1999. (*Barnaby's Picture Library*)

Futurologists tell us that we are in stage two of the consumer revolution: a shift from mass consumption to mass customisation driven by a desire to have things that fit us and our particular lifestyle exactly, and for better service. This must offer hope for small city-centre shop premises, as must the continued attraction of physical shopping, browsing and being part of a crowd: in a word, 'shoppertainment'. Another hopeful trend for towns is the growth in the number of young people postponing marriage and looking to live independently, alone, where there is a buzz, in 'swinging single cities'. Theirs is a 'flats-and-cafés' lifestyle, in contrast to the 'family suburbs', and certainly fits in with government's aim of building 60 per cent of the huge amount of new housing needed on 'brown' sites, recycled urban land. There looks to be plenty of life in the British town yet.

Birkenhead and Wirral:
An Introduction

Because of its water-bound shape, Wirral is a very easily defined area. Once-upon-a-time trees covered the whole of the peninsula and a very old quotation states that 'a squirrel could cross from the Mersey to the Dee never having to touch the earth'. After a lot of argument it seems to have been decided that the name for the area is Wirral, not *the* Wirral.

Birkenhead is now the largest town and can therefore be regarded as the capital of Wirral, which was part of Cheshire for many years, then part of Merseyside. Birkenhead has always suffered from the overpowering influence of its neighbour, Liverpool, and when the Mersey Docks & Harbour Board took over Birkenhead Docks and the Great Float, then the town lost some of its control. Because the mighty River Mersey faces the town of Birkenhead it cannot escape from being linked with the place on the other side of the water. But it has always had – and still has – its own strong identity and history. It is that which we hope to catch some glimpses of in this book. I am often asked about Birkenhead's 'nickname' – the One-eyed city. People do refer to it as that, and not always in the kindest of ways. I have heard many explanations, but none that seems plausible, so for now, for me, it's a mystery.

One of the inlets where the old ferries landed; this one is on the Liverpool side. The picture shows it in about 1860.

There are plans being put forward at the moment, and not for the first time, for a continuation of the M53 towards Hoylake, then over to Wales on a low arched bridge. There are a lot of objectors, but it would cut out the bottle-neck at Queensferry, it would save lives, by taking traffic off the New Chester Road, and it would open up both the Hoylake area and Talacre over the Dee. Isn't it strange that a lot of the objections are the same as those against opening the Mersey Railway in 1890, and identical to those against the need to build the Queensway tunnel in 1930. Times don't change that much. It's just that those who have only just arrive think they do.

As the dawn breaks on 1900 we find our town of Birkenhead in a strong growth mood. It had been a borough for over twenty years and was prospering. In 1900 the troubles of the South African war were creating extra work at the docks, which had been established fifty years earlier. The railway system on the Wirral had been completed some ten years earlier and trains ran from the town to London four or five times a day. The Birkenhead Corporation had taken over the horse-drawn trams and work was pushing ahead fast to launch Birkenhead's own electric tram system. The town was proud that it had England's first street railway (trams) and was going to be among the first to run electric 'Corporation' trams. The Mersey Railway ran under the river to Liverpool, meaning more people could commute daily to work and yet live in the more healthy rural areas around Birkenhead. The Corporation already owned and ran the Woodside Ferry which showed a fine profit each year and helped to keep rates down.

The 'Laird' influence had been good for the area. William Laird snr was the first to provide work, John was the town's first MP and John jnr the first Mayor. The shipyard was providing work for around 3,000 men and there were others, such as Graysons', who employed the same number again. John jnr had given the town a modern up-to-date hospital and a library that was the envy of many other towns. Reacting to the 1890 Bill 'Housing for the Working Classes', the Aldermen and Councillors had authorised the building of one hundred and fifty dwellings in the Egerton Street/Tunnel Road area.

The Borough motto was *Ubi Fides Ibi Lux et Robur* – 'Where There Is Faith There Is Strength and Light'. Birkenhead certainly had great faith in itself and its future at the turn of the century.

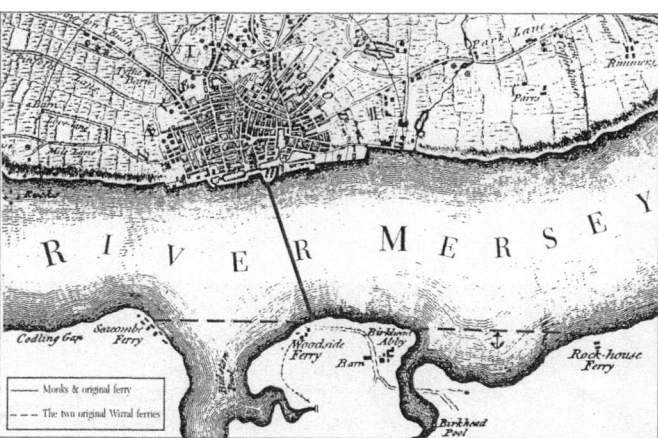

Map showing the route of the monks' ferry over the Mersey (*see* p. 47), and the routes of the two original Wirral ferries.

Birkenhead, Welcome to the Twentieth Century

The first Birkenhead boat house stood near the site of the priory, and we see it here in a watercolour of 1800.

The Mayor, Alderman T.S. Deakin, laying the foundation stone of Birkenhead Town Hall, 1883. The site had been ear-marked for the town hall since Hamilton Square had been laid out forty years earlier. William Laird had originally planned a town to rival Liverpool across the river, but money problems meant the plans had to be cut back.

A picture postcard of the town hall. Built of Scottish granite and local Storeton stone, it had cost £43,067 to build and over 5,000 people watched John Laird officially open their town hall on 10 February 1887. But the building suffered a major blow when, on 10 July 1901, fire caused the tower to come crashing down. The council rebuilt it and, I am told, used the same plans as G.O. Ellison & Sons of Liverpool who built the original. By 1903, when this postcard was issued, the town hall was back to its stylish splendour.

HAMILTON SQUARE, BIRKENHEAD.

The town hall, Hamilton Square, *c.* 1910. Hamilton Square had been named in honour of William Laird's mother, who came from Argyle in Scotland. On 27 November 1935 the town hall was again damaged by fire, which broke out in the Magistrates' Court. The Clock Tower, nearly 200ft high, was again rebuilt and this time slightly altered. The courts were refurbished and reopened in 1937, the whole repair costing £15,000.

Hamilton Sq. Birkenhead.

The lovely cross in Hamilton Square, built as a tribute to Queen Victoria. When Victoria died, the square was still owned by the people who lived in the houses around it. There were iron railings round the garden in the centre, to keep it private, and each householder had a key for their own private use of the gardens. The need for somewhere to place a memorial was one of the reasons why the town council decided to buy the square and open it up to the general public. Mr Edmund Kirby, architect, designed and supervised the building of the cross which was unveiled in 1903.

Looking down Conway Road from its corner with Argyle Street, *c.* 1905. Note the really ornate electric poles and the open-topped tram coming from Claughton Road, which you can see on the left. Our ever-present policeman stands on traffic duty and ready to help ladies cross the road.

A very early tram (no. 26), photographed outside Central station on Argyle Street South. Central station was the second underground Mersey rail station in Birkenhead. By the time of this photograph the railway had gone over to electric trains (1903) and started to put behind it the grubby years of steam trains. The 'T' on the front of the tram indicates that it's going to Tranmere. Identical tram no. 20 is now fully restored and can be found running on the new Wirral Tramway from Woodside Ferry to Taylor Street.

A close-up of the window of M.E. Hughes, confectioner, of 183 Laird Street, Birkenhead, at the start of the twentieth century. Cadburys and Frys vied with each other for trade and would decorate shops with the owners' names, along with their own advertisements, at no charge. This one has advertisements for Rowntrees and Cadburys'. Interestingly the shop was also a telephone point.

Grange Road, Birkenhead, *c*. 1920. Most of the area shown here is now pedestrianised. Again we have a policeman on duty at the Argyle cross-roads, outside the North & South Wales Bank. This end of Grange Road was near the Queensway Tunnel entrance and was partially cleared to open up the area for the road approaches. Today what is left of Grange Road (the road to the Grange) is on either side of St John's Pavement.

A fine view of Argyle Street, Birkenhead, just before the First World War. On the left is the Argyle Theatre with the Argyle public house nearer to us. The theatre was opened in December 1868 as a music hall. Dan Leno appeared there in 1870 in pantomime. George Formby snr and jnr appeared there, and so did Charlie Chaplin who received the grand sum of 30/- for a week's performances. It was at the Argyle that Harry Lauder is said to have run out of Irish songs and jokes and had to go for a second spot singing the Scottish songs that his mother had taught him. It was a huge success and his fame was for ever after assured. The theatre was bombed after the evening performance on 21 September 1940 and could not be saved.

Hamilton Street, Birkenhead, *c.* 1930. Tram no. 23 heads for Woodside Terminal from Claughton ('C' route). It has an open-ended balcony both up- and downstairs, and has been rebuilt from an earlier open-topped tram. Birkenhead scrapped its trams quite early – in 1937–38 – and before the Second World War all signs of the trams had gone from the town's street.

The bottom of Argyle Street South, looking back into Birkenhead, *c.* 1910. The tram lines go off to the right on a detour to save the trams the stiff climb up to Church Road. The gasometer on the right was part of the gas works which was bought by the Corporation in 1858. They later extended and improved the works until it eventually covered the Tranmere Pool. Next to the gas works was Yates' Castle brewery.

New Chester Road, Rock Ferry, *c.* 1920, and no. 13 tram heads for New Ferry. This is one of the original batch of single-deck trams ordered because of a low bridge on the route. After the bridge was raised the trams were made into double-deckers.

The junction of Conway Street and Argyle Street, Birkenhead, 1924. Tram no. 35 (which was twenty-three years old at the time) is on route 'CR' to Claughton Road, which was closed in 1925, making it the first tram route on Merseyside to be abandoned. Coopers Cash Chemists shop is on the left of our photograph, which was taken from where the tunnel approach fly-over is today.

The area around Woodside Ferry was an important transport cross-roads. Here, in the mid-1920s, we see no fewer than five Birkenhead Corporation trams ready to take ferry passengers onward. The building on the right is Woodside station with its five platforms and magnificent booking hall, which looked more like a baronial hall.

This is the reverse view of the picture above, taken on a day during the General Strike in 1926. Some ferries ran, staffed by management and army personnel, and some trains ran, driven by upper class volunteers who thought the workers were too 'communist' and it was therefore their duty to keep the country moving.

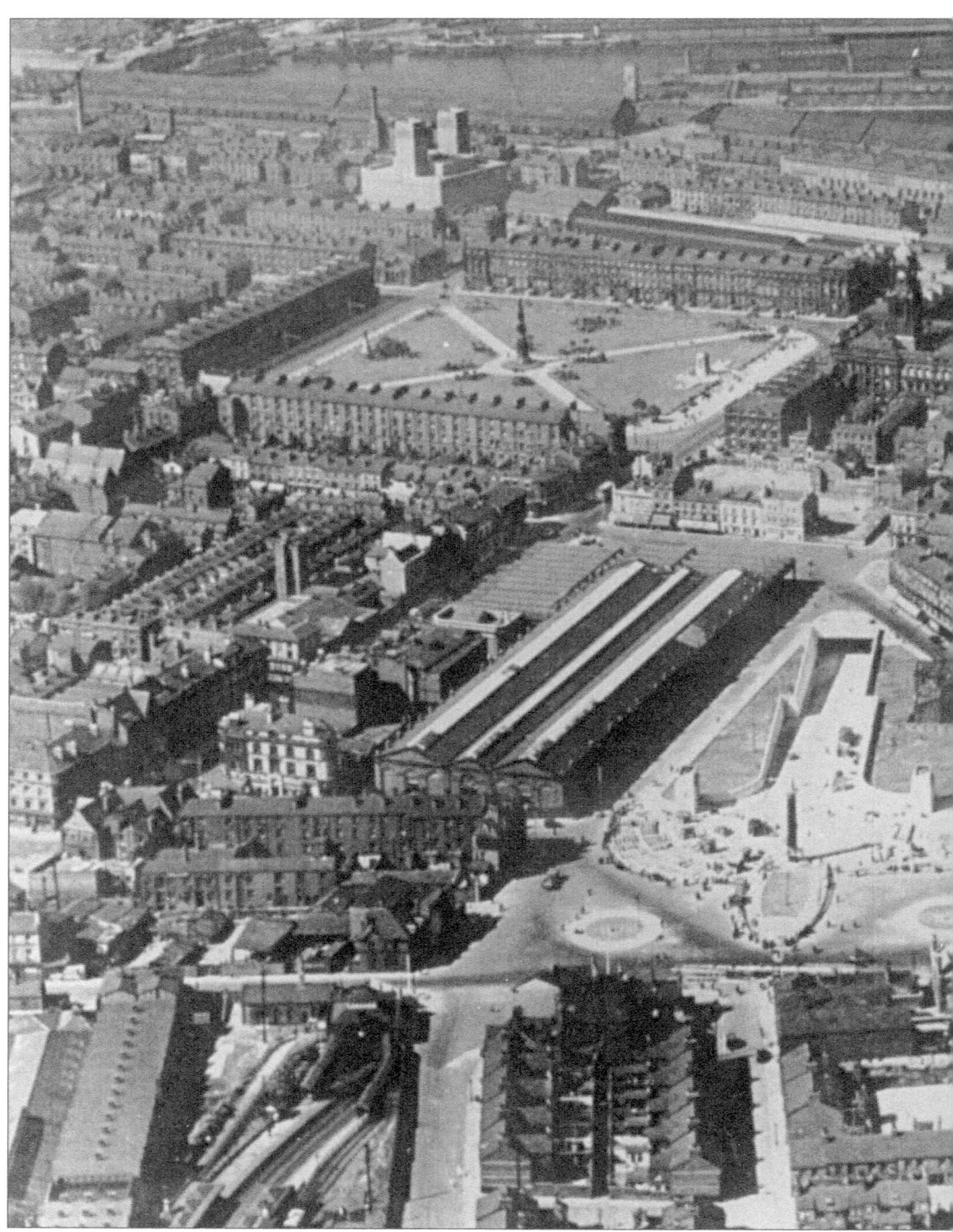

A magnificent aerial photograph of the centre of Birkenhead, *c.* 1933. In the centre of the photograph is the entrance to the Queensway Tunnel, not quite ready to open. Just left of it is the large market hall of Birkenhead's famous market. At bottom left you can see the railway lines of the GWR and these join up under Birkenhead to enter Woodside station – an inch down from the top right-hand corner.

When you consider this rail line, plus the underground Mersey Railway that runs from Hamilton Square station to Birkenhead Central and onward, as well as the Queensway Tunnel and its forgotten dock branch, there is an amazing amount of tunnels and underground workings below Birkenhead.

Woodside ventilation station, built to pump air into and out · of the Queensway Tunnel, shows up clear and new at the top left of the picture. Herbert J. Rowse was the architect and, although we take it for granted now, it won a bronze medal from the Royal Institute of British Architects. Take your time, get out a magnifying glass, for this is a picture to savour.

27

The Mayor of Birkenhead meets the Mayor of Liverpool during the construction of the Mersey Road Tunnel in April 1933. Opened by King George V on 18 July 1934, it proved an instant success. One unforeseen side-effect was that shops in Birkenhead reported a downturn in sales of luxury goods as people could drive through the tunnel and shop in Liverpool where there was more choice.

The plan for the tunnel had been raised by Liverpool as early as 1922. Parliamentary permission was obtained in August 1925, but it only gave authority to collect tolls for twenty years (later increased to twenty-five years). Work started on 16 December 1925 and the original plan saw trams running in the bottom half of the tunnel with the roadway above.

After it opened people were so interested in vehicles emerging from under the river that a crowd would gather each evening just to watch, as we see here in a picture from September 1934. Major problems that had to be solved included the re-routing of gas mains, phone lines, electric cables and the main sewer. In addition, hundreds of people had to be rehoused as their homes, and the central library, were all demolished to make way for the tunnel entrance.

Grange Road, Birkenhead – a later version of the photograph on page 22. The Grange Hotel, owned and managed by Birkenhead Breweries, stands out well on the left of the picture. This company was formed on 29 August 1865 when two local family brewing firms decided to amalgamate. The Aspinal family brewed at Cleveland Street, Birkenhead, and the Cooks at Oxton Road, Birkenhead, – together they went forward to become the longest- established brewers in the area. 'BB' Stout was one of their great successes and became popular with visitors on holiday in the area.

The Cleveland Street brewery stopped production after being bombed during the Second World War. However, it was quickly re-built and was producing beer for the 'heroes' again after only eleven weeks.

The milling of flour was one of Birkenhead's biggest industries. There were more mills in Birkenhead than anywhere else in Great Britain. 'Spillers' was just one of the many companies which had sited their mills near the Birkenhead Float, where ships from Canada and Australia would dock to unload their precious cargoes of grain. This meant that Birkenhead was a target for German bombers during the Second World War and suffered repeated bombing raids in a bid to stop production of flour for bread and other vital foodstuffs.

Buchanan's flour mill after it had been destroyed during a bombing raid in March 1941.

Over two thousand houses were destroyed or damaged beyond repair in Birkenhead during the conflict. The council put together five hundred pre-fabricated houses towards the end of the war to help with the desperate housing shortage.

Rowland's Garage, Ullet Road, Birkenhead (later Cubbin & North). It was bombed on 5 September 1940. Believe it or not, there were cars under the rubble and they were all right for sale after the rubble was removed and they were cleaned up!

Bomb damage in Birkenhead's shopping area after the raid of 1 October 1940. Over a thousand people died in air raids on Wirral during the Second World War and Merseyside was the most heavily bombed area after London.

Birkenhead docks took a lot of punishment in the Second World War. Here we see American tanks being unloaded after the US had been dragged into the fight against Hitler's Germany.

Steam locomotives from Vulcan Foundries, Newton-le-Willows, near Warrington, being loaded for Burma. The docks between Birkenhead and Wallasey were run by the Mersey Docks & Harbour Board and were therefore controlled from Liverpool – a point that sometimes rankled with local people.

A rare photograph of the defences constructed at the mouth of the River Mersey. These forts were built just off New Brighton and were the last line of defence for the Mersey. At the mouth of the river were two large minefields and ships came and went by hugging the Welsh coast line, past Rhyl and then Wirral. Any other approach to the Mersey led through the minefields.

A steam ship coaling at Birkenhead Docks in the mid-1930s. Because of the docks there was plenty of work for the people of Birkenhead, Wallasey and all over Wirral. Numbers employed are always hard to calculate as the service industries to the docks were unregulated. Ships needed coal, food, repair, cleaning, painting, etc., and these services provided many jobs.

An aerial view of the Birkenhead Docks which provided so much work for over a century. At bottom right you can see the graving docks of the Grayson Rollo & Clover Docks Co., who were at one time just as busy as Cammell Laird's. Hamilton Square is to the left and of course Wallasey is at the top of our picture.

The new council flats, Eldon Gardens and Oak Gardens, constructed in the 1950s (the first tenants moved in in 1956) to ease the post-war housing problems. They were eleven storeys high and at the time were thought to be the answer to the question of future housing.

Here, shops, stores and pedestrians on Grange Road West, Birkenhead, are captured on a pleasant morning in the mid-1950s. It is probably a Sunday because there are so few people about. People could, and did, go out on a Sunday 'window shopping' – the days of steel shutters and fortified shops were still a long way off. (*Liverpool Daily Post & Echo*)

Another glimpse of Grange Road, Birkenhead, 13 November 1967. Shops included Marcel Fashions, Jackson the Tailors and Norvic Shoes as well as Martins the Cleaners, giving the shoppers plenty of choice.

After the war everything struggled to get back to normal. Building materials were in short supply and petrol was the same. Here we see a Birkenhead Corporation bus no. 154 running down Hamilton Street to Woodside in about 1948. Petrol prices are displayed outside the garage: 5/- for the top of the range. Prices did not change so fast in those days, which is why they could be painted on the wall with certainty. Today this area is again under development. (*Liverpool Daily Post & Echo*)

A lovely photograph of Grange Road, the hub of Birkenhead's shopping district, caught in November 1956. Everyone knew where their favourite shops were and there was plenty of choice. It was not long before this kind of shopping was to disappear from our larger towns when schemes were passed for shopping centres which were all under cover. Today the left side of the picture is covered by the Pyramid Centre and St John's Pavement – a great improvement from when we had to shop outside in all weathers, but it did mean the loss of many small shops and businesses. (*Liverpool Daily Post & Echo*)

A 1950s photograph of the tunnel approaches in Birkenhead. This area was officially named King's Square, but most people seemed to have forgotten the name as it is never used today. The tunnel is 2.13 miles from entrance to exit and is 36ft wide kerb to kerb. Over 560,000lb of explosives were used to blast through the rock to move the 1,200,000 tons of rubble cut out. Some 82,000 tons of cast iron were used to line the tunnel and up to 4,300 gallons of water were pumped out every minute during construction. When the tunnel opened there was a speed limit of 21mph in the slow lane and 30mph in the fast lane. It is still an offence to drive at less than 6mph in the slow lane, or to turn off your engine and coast downhill to the tunnel's lowest point.

A composite card of Birkenhead from the early 1960s. It is worth studying for the view of Clifton Crescent (bottom right) showing the area just before it was redeveloped for the flyovers and new traffic systems. The postcard must have been put together by someone outside the area because Bidston parish church does not really fit in with Birkenhead. Much better would have been St Mary's, Birkenhead's parish church and the old priory.

A view of central Birkenhead in the 1960s. The tower of the Mersey underground railway system dominates the foreground; note the four chimneys, one in each corner of the ornate tower. Hamilton Square itself is in the middle of the picture, with the war memorial and the cross almost at the centre. The new block of offices over on the right can be seen quite clearly – the grime of the smoky 1960s has not had time to blend it into the rest of Birkenhead.

A late 1960s view of the tunnel entrance. The market and houses and warehouses around the top of the entrance can be seen. The toll for a car through the tunnel has just gone up again and there is talk of selling off the tunnels to a private company. It is a far cry from the original ideal of free crossings once the initial outlay had been repaid. In the 1950s and 1960s there was a charge for each passenger. I can remember an uncle of mine making me and my cousin duck down and get under a blanket to save two bob on the way to New Brighton, and then giving us the shilling each to spend when we got there.

A view of the area alongside Woodside in the late 1950s, showing the 280ft chimney that dominated the area. The Pier Hotel is the white building to the left and Woodside taxis wait below the mill chimney.

Building Great Ships

An aerial view of the Cammell Laird shipyard in 1960. Situated on the banks of a great river, Birkenhead seems a natural place for a ship building industry. The first ships were not built on the banks of the Mersey, but in the more sheltered waters of the Float (River Birket) which had long been used by local shipping as a place to shelter from storms. The River Dee was once an important seaway and Chester was the first port in the area. The Romans had sailed up the Dee and anchored at Chester (Deva) a thousand years before any development of ports on the River Mersey began.

William Laird arrived in Birkenhead in about 1824. He set up business as a boat builder in the same year that the Liverpool & Birmingham Railway put forward plans for a rail line under the Mersey to connect the two cities. William concerned himself with the matters of his adopted home and pushed for Commissioners to run Birkenhead and develop it. He moved his works to the river bank, its present position, in 1856, after Birkenhead Docks opened in 1847.

Cammell Laird were not the only ship builders in Birkenhead. Today we seem to forget Grayson Rollo & Clover Docks Co., an amalgamation whose history goes back even further. It developed into a repair and refit company (rather than building ships), and was taken into the Laird group in 1962. It was Laird's who turned out the great ships *The Alabama*, *Ark Royal*, *Thetis* and *Mauretania*, each one with its own fascinating story. The name Cammell Laird and the names of these great ships are etched into the town's history for ever. Above we see the yard from the Tranmere oil jetty in the late 1950s. (*Inset*) John Laird MP, son of William Laird, the founder of the company.

Windsor Castle receives admiring glances from the large crowd at Cammell Laird's shipyard who are waiting to see it launched on 28 June 1959 by HM the Queen Mother. The 38,000-ton liner was built for the Union Castle Steamship Company and she spent many years on the South Africa run as well as cruising in the winter months from Southampton.

Men leaving work at Cammell Laird shipyard, 1946. During the war the yard had been at full stretch, building and repairing ships. Between September 1939 and September 1945 Laird's built 106 fighting ships, one every twenty days on average. At the time of this photograph there were 15,000 men on the books at the yard, most of them skilled. During the 1950s and 1960s the workforce (along with the dockers) got a bad name for strikes and union 'work-to-rules'. One such incident was a three-month strike from 16 March to 5 June 1964, when 1,200 workers struck for a 1/- per hour rise for the shipwrights. Today the yard seems to be gathering work once more, albeit under different names and guises, but the skills of the workforce which were allowed to slip away will be a lot harder to bring back. (*Liverpool Daily Post & Echo*)

A view of the no. 1 and no. 2 jetties in the south slipway around 1970. The jetty in the middle was constructed in 1964 after the yard won the contract for two Polaris submarines in 1963. Interestingly you can see the houses that were left standing as the shipyard spread – they were used for keeping stores and some of the more expensive tackle. (*David Roberts*)

It must have been quite exciting to pull into Woodside railway station and see these ocean giants right next to you. Just how close they were can be seen from this picture of a bulk-carrier in the dry dock. The station looks deserted – it could be after 1967, when it closed, and it may be awaiting demolition. I once spent three months working on a ship in this dry dock, getting the printer's shop ready for sea on the SS *Ocean Monarch*. To a seaman, working in dry dock was a horrible experience. The ship has no water or toilets, only emergency lights and no power for cooking, or making tea, and was always very dirty. (*Liverpool Daily Post & Echo*)

The launch of HM Submarine *Revenge* in 1967. The keel of no. 1317 had been laid in 1965 and the Polaris submarine was handed over completely fitted out in 1969. The firm was revamped at the start of the Polaris years and the Cammell Laird Group formed. I think the people standing on the sub's deck deserve a medal for bravery for just being there while it goes into the water for the very first time! (*David Roberts*)

Cammell Laird's have built some quite unusual things over the last 150 years. Parts of the Mulberry harbours used on D-Day were constructed in Birkenhead. Here we see a floating dry dock being taken out into the river for trials. It would be partially submerged, then driven under the ship that was to be repaired. Then air would be pumped in and the dock and ship inside would rise to the surface so work could begin. The sail ship behind is one of the training ships that were anchored on the river over the years.

There were quite a few other manufacturing industries in and around Birkenhead. The Revo-Luxe cooker was made on Wirral before Candy started its fridge and washing machine business on the New Chester Road. Above, right, we see two white-coated technicians (that is how they were referred to at the time) spot-welding a deluxe kitchen cabinet in 1934 – just the thing for a modern kitchen. Right, we have an advertisement, *c.* 1930, for Vernon Toys. Although the address on the advertisement is Liverpool, they were made in Birkenhead. The company were delighted when the Shah of Persia ordered a car for his son, and they spent years telling everyone about the deal.

Kiddies love –

—these exciting toys. Soundly constructed of steel and aluminium, they will stand up to the roughest of use.

Write for leaflet No. T. 54.

Vernon Toys
REG NO. 847221

VERNONS INDUSTRIES LIMITED LIVERPOOL

Ferry 'cross the Mersey

The large, cluttered landing stage at Woodside in 1959, before refurbishment. (*Len Jackson*). The history of the ferry is well documented. The monks settled at Birkenhead in 1150. They rowed people across the Mersey, as well as taking their vegetables and herbs (medicines) to various markets up and down the river. In 1317 they applied for, and were granted, permission to charge for the services that they gave to travellers, like food and lodging, and taking them across the river, etc. By 1330 they employed auxiliaries to carry on the river crossing service on their behalf, and this lasted until Henry VIII shut down the monasteries. The 'rights of ferry' were sold and changed hands many times until the Birkenhead Commissioners acquired the 'rights' in 1842 and ran a service for over one hundred years. After the granting of permission to form a Corporation in Birkenhead in 1877, the ferry was handed over to the Corporation in 1879 and then, in 1969, the Mersey Passenger Transport Authority and Executive was set up and they took over the buses and ferries from Birkenhead, Wallasey and Liverpool Corporations.

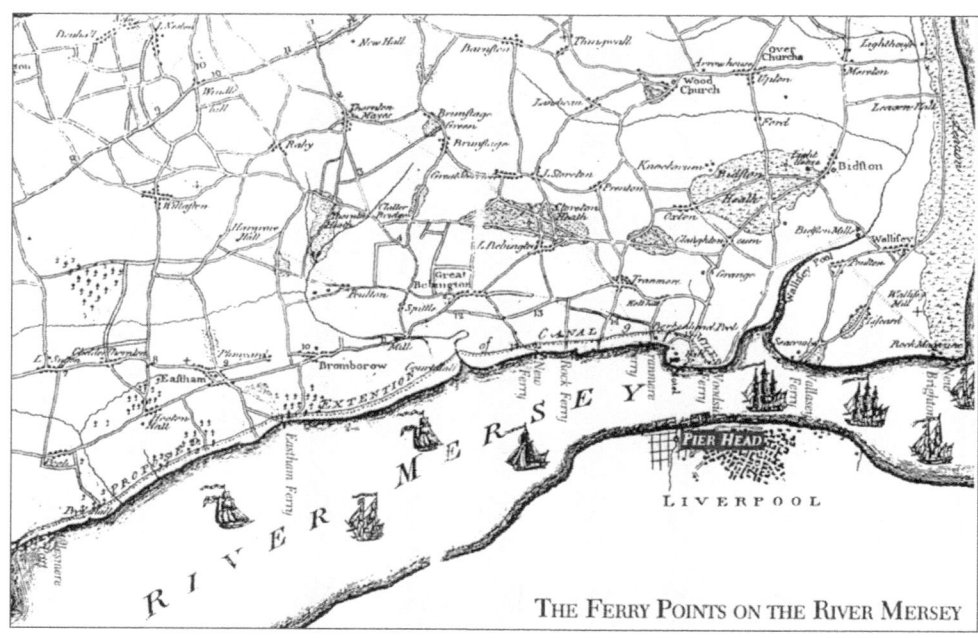

THE FERRY POINTS ON THE RIVER MERSEY

ETNA, TRANMERE FERRY
Steam Packet.

THIS Packet (as was originally intended) will commence running from the New Slip, at the west side of the Queen's Dock Graving Docks, on Thursday Morning, the 17th April, at Eight o'Clock, where every convenience will be found for taking on board and discharging Horses and Cattle of every description going to and from Cheshire, without the trouble that has hitherto been experienced in the common Sail Boats, and which it is the intention of the Proprietors as much as possible to obviate. This Vessel remaining at each side only Ten Minutes, the certainty with which Passengers may calculate upon crossing, at all times of the day, will be an advantage that never yet has been afforded to those whose business or pleasure lead them to cross the River.—The Fares for Passengers, &c. will be precisely the same as customary by other regular Boats. Due notice will be given when Carts and Carriages of every description will be conveyed over, which will be in a very few days.

Performed by BATMAN, FRENCH & Co.

April 15th, 1817.

In order to get two fees instead of one, Henry VIII decided that the 'right to ferry' people from Seacome to Woodside, Birkenhead, should have a separate licence from the one covering the Woodside to Liverpool crossing. It was this split in 1544 that led to there being two corporations running the ferries in the nineteenth century. Above is a map showing the extent of the ferry service at its largest. There were ferries at Eastham, New Ferry, Rock Ferry and Tranmere up river from Woodside, and Wallasey and New Brighton down river. Before the ship canal was built in 1895, ferries would also run to Ellesmere Port and Runcorn.

A poster for a steam boat on the ferry service of its then owners Batman, French & Co. It was a strange craft and looked like two boats stuck together with a single paddle wheel in the middle. It worked, however, and from this time onwards the ferries became more regulated and the services expanded.

The Ferry, Birkenhead

The postcard above shows the floating terminal at Woodside. As a child I used to think it was magic that sometimes the tunnel down to the ferry was very steep and at other times it was almost level.

In 1886, when Mersey Rail opened, people said that it would be the end of the ferry service but steam trains were not well suited to running under the Mersey and the tunnels were always full of smoke and dirt. The ferries hit back by advertising themselves as the 'Healthy Way to Cross' and the slogan has stayed with them ever since.

When electric trains took over in 1903 it was said again that this would be the end for the ferries and the warning was repeated in 1934 when the road tunnel opened. Neither prediction proved to be true, thank goodness! In 1938 the ferry advert ran: 'You can be taken to Liverpool cramped in a car, squashed on a bus, or take a constitutional round the deck of a Birkenhead Ferry, have a cup of tea and arrive at your office invigorated and refreshed.' No contest! The advertisement on the right is from the 1950s.

BIRKENHEAD CORPORATION FERRIES

TRAVEL BY THE "HEALTH" ROUTE
via

WOODSIDE FERRY
(LIVERPOOL AND BIRKENHEAD)

CHEAP THROUGH RETURN FARES

by Woodside Ferry Day Boats and Corporation Motor Bus to and from Liverpool Landing Stage 5d. and 6d. according to bus stage, also return tickets from 8d. to 1/4 to and from other parts of Wirral

Tickets are issued subject to Bye-laws, Rules and Regulations of the Corporation vide notices

LIST OF SEASON TICKET RATES ON APPLICATION TO:
R. S. COWAN, M.I.Mar.E. *General Manager*
WOODSIDE, BIRKENHEAD

Woodside landing stage seen from a ferry, *c.* 1920. The Birkenhead Commissioners decided to name their boats after areas of the town and this tradition continues today. There have been three *Woodsides*, three *Bebingtons* and *Claughtons* and four *Birkenheads*. There have been four ships called *Mersey*, two called *Liverpool* and two each called *Lancashire* and *Cheshire*. The *Mountwood*, *Woodchurch* and *Overchurch* were the ships that kept the service going through the 1980s and 1990s, but the *Mountwood* was, early in 2000, renamed the *Royal Daffodil* after a refit. This brings us to the two famous Wallasey ferries, *Iris* and *Daffodil*, which went into war service in 1914 and took part in a heroic action at Zeebrugge. Upon their return, the King wrote to Wallasey saying that they could be renamed *Royal Iris* and *Royal Daffodil*. The Wallasey Corporation has, for the most part, always had flower names for its boats and has never repeated one. The first one was the *Water Lily* and others include *Wild Rose*, *Sunflower*, *Blue Bell*, *Daisy* and *Violet*. More unusual choices include *Shamrock*, *Pansy* and *Thistle*.

Wherever the ferry boat piers were constructed a whole industry rose up, catering for the travellers and day trippers. Here we see the Ferry Hotel at Eastham, built just after the Eastham pier opened in the mid-1850s. There were gardens at the side of the hotel and a century ago it was a treat to take the ferry and stroll through Eastham Gardens. The ornate arch was set up to commemorate Queen Victoria's Jubilee in 1897.

Eastham Ferry *c.* 1900, and you can just make out a little of the Victoria Jubilee Arch behind the trees. Eastham Gardens really were a big attraction and the tea rooms and Eastham Ferry Hotel were very popular. Eastham, mentioned in the Domesday Book as East Hamlet, was at one time the main crossing point for stage- coach passengers from Chester, who transferred to sailing ships here for the last part of their journey to Liverpool.

Eastham ferry and pier, 1906. The tide is low and the crowd of passengers face quite a climb from the boat. The place was so popular that, in 1912, a company was formed to take over the ferry and the gardens. It was called the New Liverpool, Eastham Ferry & Hotel Co. Ltd but became a victim of its own success – because it was so crowded, middle-class families started to stay away! The gardens became thought of as 'common and vulgar' and the service soon went downhill. It finally closed in 1929 and the pier was dismantled shortly after.

51

Looking down Bedford Road towards the Ferry Terminal at Rock Ferry, 1919. The terminal opened in about 1831 as part of a new Liverpool–Rock Ferry–New Ferry service. It was a workers' service at its height, enabling office workers in the early 1900s to move out here and yet work in Liverpool. The tunnel, and increased bus services, killed this ferry off. It closed in 1939, just as the clouds of war were gathering.

The esplanade at Rock Ferry, *c.* 1900. A stroll along the wide front and a seat in the ornate Victorian shelter must have been attractive to courting couples. Rock Park, which gave the area its name, lies just behind the trees. Though the ferry service has closed, the pier is still there today, used as a tank cleaning and discharging point for ships. You can still promenade on the esplanade.

Trains, Boats
and Trams

A sketch of the proposed 1844 bridge over the River Mersey. Once a steam ferry service became feasible the development of Wirral, or at least the Mersey side, began. As people moved to the south side of the River Mersey so the task of getting them from Wirral to Liverpool and back became big business. As early as 1844 there were plans for a road bridge to cross the river. That plan seemed to falter as no one could decide how high it should be to let ships past. There were later plans for a bridge like the Britannia Bridge over the Menai Straits at Anglesey but the approaches at Birkenhead proved too troublesome and the plans were dropped. In 1922 Liverpool Council paid for a study and, together with Birkenhead and Wallasey, set up a committee to look at the merits of a road bridge or road tunnel across the river. The study said that a road bridge would look attractive but would cost around £6.5m, would be very vulnerable in times of war and would pose difficulties in times of high winds and storms. The bridge idea was dropped once again.

It is an oft-quoted fact that in 1860 Birkenhead had England's first tram. George Train persuaded the Commissioners to let him dig up part of the road and he laid railway lines along the streets. These were at first called 'street railways', for that is what they were, but the name soon changed to 'tram carriages' and then 'trams'. Above we see one of the early horse-drawn trams run by the United Tramway & Omnibus Co. Ltd, 'omnibus' here referring to the horse-drawn wagonettes that ran at the time. United was one of three companies who ran the four routes around the town.

An early Birkenhead Corporation double-decker bus. As early as 1925 Leyland started making 'Leviathans', double-deckers with covered tops. Birkenhead ordered the first eight to be built. They had open stairways at the back. This is probably a Leyland Leviathan from the 1927 batch with its enclosed stairs – a great advance at the time. At first it ran with solid tyres as it was thought to be too heavy for pneumatic ones but, as tyre technology improved, the solid tyres were replaced.

A Mersey Railway electric train pauses at Birkenhead Park station while the driver and conductor have their photograph taken in the 1920s. The fact that the unit looks American is due to the fact that a lot of it was. The steam train which first ran had proved too dirty and the line had gone into receivership. The board and the receivers were looking for some way to electrify the line but they had no money. Contact was made with George Westinghouse, an American who had a factory in Trafford Park, Manchester. George was the only one who could get them out of this mess – and he did. He paid off their debts, electrified the line within two years and kept the steam trains going until the electric system was ready. His only stipulation was that all electrical equipment, bogies and generating equipment be made at his factory in Chicago. The whole tunnel was white-washed end to end and the stations cleaned up. Passengers liked the new clean look and the fast service, and soon Mersey Rail went into profit and George Westinghouse got his money back. The Chicago-style units lasted until 1956, and they were designed so that five-car units could be operated in peak times as shown below. This 1930s photograph was also taken at Birkenhead Park station, which opened in 1888.

A rare picture of the electric unit trials on the Wirral railway. Taken at Hoylake station, it shows electric train 28678 on trial with the driver learning how to handle the new unit. Alongside it you can see the back of a steam train travelling the other way, towards Birkenhead. This picture was taken on 5 March 1938 and the last steam train on this line ran on 13 March 1938, just eight days later.

Birkenhead Central station on the Mersey Railway, *c.* 1908. There are two units in the station and another two in stabling area sheds on the right. Under the tunnel the trains were controlled by lights but here, where the line comes to the surface, we see normal signals. Birkenhead Central station opened on 1 February 1886.

Tram no. 56 in Prenton Road West, 30 September 1934. This was the end of the line in more ways than one for the Birkenhead to Prenton route, service 'P', which ceased operations on this day. The bottom half of this tram became a shelter in Arrowe Park for about thirty years.

Laird Street tram junction, Birkenhead – a busy scene, c. 1910. Tram no. 19, built in 1901 by G.F. Milnes, a Birkenhead company, is on the Oxton circular route. Here it is turning into Mallaby Street on its way back to Woodside. The gates on the extreme right of the picture lead into the Corporation's Laird Street tram depot.

Buses and trams mix easily at Woodside, 1933. Tram no. 23 waits to leave for Claughton via Conway Road. It is an open-ended balcony type and behind it a Birkenhead bus has just arrived from Port Sunlight, Old Chester Road and Lower Bebington, route 50. It is a Leyland 'Titan', bought by the Corporation in 1930. (*M.J. O'Connor*)

BIRKENHEAD CORPORATION
TRANSPORT

FIRST TRAMWAY IN EUROPE   -   -   1860
FINEST MOTOR OMNIBUS SERVICES TODAY

The Corporation Transport Services cover all parts of the Borough and surrounding districts including :

NEW BRIGHTON, EGREMONT, LISCARD, WALLASEY, SEACOMBE, MORETON, LEASOWE, FRANKBY, GREASBY, CALDY, HESWALL, THURSTASTON, IRBY, EASTHAM FERRY, EASTHAM VILLAGE, BROM-BOROUGH VILLAGE, BROMBOROUGH POOL, PORT SUNLIGHT, LOWER BEBINGTON, NEW FERRY, SPITAL CROSS ROADS (for Raby Mere) AND HIGHER BEBINGTON

Convenient for Business or Pleasure
Comfortable Travelling and Low Fares

The Corporation are prepared to supply Special Buses on Hire for Picnic Parties, Weddings and other functions. Terms on application to the General Manager.

Time-Tables are issued at intervals at a charge of 2d. Route Maps issued free.
Telephone : Birkenhead 3070, 3071, 3072

Transport Offices   G. A. Cherry
LAIRD STREET, BIRKENHEAD   *General Manager*

Oh, how we long for the days when buses were run by the Corporation! There was a pride in being on time and sticking to the timetable. The options were simple – Corporation buses for local trips and Crosville or Ribble buses for long journeys.

A Wallasey Corporation bus waiting at the Seacombe Hotel end of the Wallasey bus station, mid-1950s. The bus was painted in the sea-green and cream livery of the Corporation. (*R.H.G. Simpson*)

A Birkenhead bus in Hamilton Street on the 79 route out to Arrowe, Irby and Thurstaston. The bus is a Leyland 'Titan' bought in 1960. (*R.H.G. Simpson*)

Woodside bus station, looking away from the ferry terminal. The Mersey Railway Tower can be seen in the background. The bus is again a Leyland 'Titan', bought in 1950, which lasted until 1973. (*R.H.G. Simpson*)

GWR tank engine no.
3571 leaving Woodside
railway station with a local
passenger train, 1930.
(*Locofotos*)

Locomotive no. 3216 waits
to leave Woodside with
an express destined for
Paddington, London, 1930.
The large copper dome and
sloping boiler of the engine
are very distinctive and, as
you can see, the drivers and
firemen were very open to
the elements. (*Locofotos*)

Locomotive no. 6649 backs
out of Woodside station
after being relieved of its
carriages on a local Chester
(stopping) train, 1930.
(*Locofotos*)

Locomotive no. 6649 ready to run, tender first, on a local service, 1930s. The station and its platforms were below the outside street level because it was simpler for the line, which had come under Birkenhead, to stay on the level rather than climb steeply for the last quarter mile. (*Locofotos*)

An overall view of Woodside station, April 1930. Because the five platforms were set low the station did not dominate the Woodside area as much as it could have done. Locomotive no. 6894 waits, light engine, while behind is GWR no. 3751. (*Locofotos*)

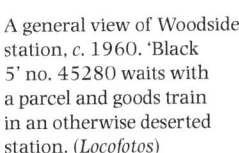

A general view of Woodside station, *c.* 1960. 'Black 5' no. 45280 waits with a parcel and goods train in an otherwise deserted station. (*Locofotos*)

The staff line up at Neston station for their photograph, *c.* 1909. It opened as Neston & Parkgate station in 1896 and was then renamed Neston North and later Neston. The line was part of the Great Central Railway Company at this time.

Hoylake railway station in the early years of the twentieth century. From 1866, when the station opened, until 1876 this was the end of the line. On 1 April 1876 an extension to West Kirby opened. A steam train is shunting goods wagons at the far end of the station and thoughts of electrification (1938) are far away.

An Edwardian view of Hoylake station (including gasometer behind). One of the staff is taking a risk, crossing the line with a train approaching.

A 2–6–0 Great Western engine passes through Hooton station with a long goods train, mid-1930s. The sign on the platform tells travellers this is the junction for Neston, Parkgate, Heswall, etc. Hooton station opened in 1844.

LMS 'Crab' no. 42727 waits with a goods train at Hooton station in the late 1950s. Because Hooton had two branch lines there was a lot of goods traffic through the station, especially on the Helsby branch line.

The Manchester Ship Canal actually started at Eastham on Wirral. When construction was taking place in the 1890s it interfered with some of the old established ports and ferry points but by the time the canal opened officially in 1894, things had settled down. (Above) a sailing ship in the sea lock at Eastham with a paddle ship heading up the canal in 1902. (Below) the same scene twenty-five years later, and a very over-loaded tramp steamer with its cargo of wood has been raised to the level of the canal ready for its onward journey, probably to Runcorn.

The Borough of Wallasey

The village, Wallasey, as it was in the mid-1930s. The Borough of Wallasey was incorporated in 1910, and consisted of the following: New Brighton, Wallasey Village, Liscard, Egremont, Poulton, Moreton, Seacombe, Leasowe and Saughall Massie. Wallasey owes its name to Wirral's proximity to Wales, and it was known in the past as *Wala-s-eg* – 'Island of the Welsh' and *Wala tun* – 'Fortified farm where Welsh live'.

In 1911 a census declared 78,514 people lived in the borough, though it did not get a Member of Parliament until 1918. Wallasey was larger than Birkenhead, being 9,216 acres to Birkenhead's 8,598 acres, and though older it lived in the shadow of its more important twin. Wallasey is altogether different from its neighbour Birkenhead, which grew – controlled and planned – into a town. The Borough of Wallasey brought together a collection of urban district councils for ease of administration. Each of those areas has retained much of its own individuality. The motto chosen for this new Wallasey is *Audemus dum Cavemus*, 'We are bold, whilst we are cautious', which gives much food for thought.

Wallasey Village has kept its charm and old worldliness even though there have been redevelopments. Here is a postcard, *c.* 1910, showing off 'A Bit of Old Wallasey'. Holiday-makers could catch an electric train or tram up to Wallasey Village and spend a pleasant day exploring an old part of Wirral. They could climb Bidston Hill, enjoy an ice cream or walk down to Harrison Park. Don't forget that people came to New Brighton for their annual two weeks' holiday and they wouldn't expect to lie on the beach in the sunshine every day.

Wallasey Village, looking down Leasowe Road towards Leasowe itself. This photograph was taken in the very late 1930s and traffic is scarce: as well as the car in the centre of the road, there is another at the petrol station on the left. A petrol station still stands on this site today. Can you make out the railway bridge in the distance?

Although you enter Wallasey once you have crossed four bridges and the float, to get to Old Wallasey or Wallasey Village you have to travel a few more miles. Even today the centre of the village is not a single road or street but just an area called Wallasey Village which starts at Harrison Drive and goes up to Breck Road. The original caption on this postcard was 'The Village, Wallasey' but the view shown is right down at the bottom of the village and technically is Harrison Drive down by Grove Road station. I suppose 'The Village' is quainter and would sell more postcards in the early 1930s when it was published.

A 1920s view of Wallasey Village, from Grove Road station. A policeman looks in vain for some traffic to control. This part looks far more built-up and has the air of a more commercially aware district. The bank on the right is now a day nursery and the shops opposite have lost their verandahs.

Old Cottage, Breck Road, Wallasey. Breck Road is a continuation of the Village. Breck is an old Norse word for ridge or slope and the road does slope upwards, a fact that is compounded by Cliff Road running off at the top.

The Old Cheshire Cheese Inn, Wallasey, *c*. 1890. One thing we tend to forget today is that Wirral and all its surrounding areas were traditionally part of the county of Cheshire. A hundred and fifty years ago this area looked south to Chester for its administrative decisions, not across the water to the 'Pool'. The inn was rebuilt about sixty years ago, but it is still there today.

The Borough of Wallasey has over 7 miles of beach around its coastline. Sometimes old postcards would mislabel one part of the borough, say Egremont as Wallasey or New Brighton, but this one seems to be where it says – New Promenade, Wallasey. There is an American Soda Fountain kiosk and of course a place to buy tea, and it does not look too warm either as everybody seems well covered up.

A composite card of Wallasey, with photographs from all over the area. Vale Park is near New Brighton Pier and Central Park is over in Liscard. Warren Park and Harrison Drive are of course in New Brighton. The centre photograph shows the old parish church, St Hilary's, at Wallasey Village. This church dates back to the sixth century. The tower standing separate from the main body of the church dates from 1530 and was all that was left after a fire. Twice more the church has burnt down and the towers collapsed, hence the saying 'Thrice burned, twice a church without a tower, once a tower without a church'. The tower still stands.

A 1920s view of Harrison Drive at New Brighton/Wallasey, looking down towards the front and 'Mock Beggar Wharf'. The Harrison family gave the land for a park just the other side of the railway and that park and this part of the drive were named after them. King's Parade is a little further on. Wallasey golf course and a miniature golf course are on the left.

Liscard Road, Liscard, looking down away from Liscard Village, probably in the early 1920s. One reason why there are so many people about is the presence of Central Park on the right. At 56 acres it was the largest of Wallasey's parks and boasted a grand boating lake.

Liscard, Wallasey, in the 1960s, showing the roundabout and looking into the road called Liscard Village. The shops and buildings on the left were part of Liscard's cinema, which opened in 1926 as the Capitol showing *Midnight Sun*. The 1,390 seats were full, and the £22 raised went to Victoria Central Hospital. At the time of our photograph it was the ABC Cinema and had just undergone a two-month closure for a complete modernisation. The name Liscard is said to be Celtic and means 'The court on the cliff', and is first recorded as *Lisenecark*.

71

Liscard, *c.* 1905. The tram lines had not long been laid and the poles supporting the wires are the early decorative style. Note the uniform of the policeman on duty outside the bank at the cross-roads.

Liscard roundabout in 1964. The bank is there on the right and we can see the cinema, which was the ABC Carlton by then but had opened in 1926 as the Capitol. In 1973 the owners wanted to convert it to a bingo hall downstairs and a cinema upstairs. The council insisted on lifts to the top floor and safety measures which the company thought too expensive and the place closed down. The last film shown was *Take Me High* by Cliff Richard. It was four years before it opened as a bingo hall, and it still operates as such today.

The Promenade, Seacombe, *c.* 1912. The long jetty is Egremont pier. This was the longest of all the Mersey ferry piers because of the shallow rocky shore. The one in this picture was constructed in 1909. Unfortunately it was hit by an oil tanker in 1932 and closed for a year for repairs. In 1941, during a black out, it was hit again and this time there were no repairs and the floating landing stage was taken away and used elsewhere. The pier itself was removed altogether in 1949. New Brighton tower can be seen on the skyline.

Every seaside place has to have one of these photographs of waves crashing against the sea wall in a wintry scene. This is Seacombe, taken in 1935 for a newspaper feature. (*Liverpool Daily Post & Echo*)

Old Mother Redcap's Inn stood between Seacombe and Rock Point. The inn (which was pulled down in the 1970s) had a sign showing the grand old lady who was said to be a friend of the pirates and ship-wreckers of Wirral. Sailors would leave their gold, silver and valuables with her when they went away to sea. It is said that her hidden treasure is still there somewhere, waiting to be found.

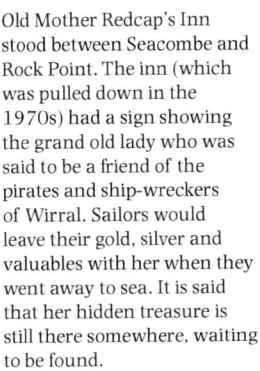

King Street, Egremont, looking towards New Brighton, *c.* 1920. Church Street is the road on the left and the way down to Egremont ferry is on the right. The tram in the picture is a Wallasey one on route 'S' (Seabank Road). King's Road was the direct route from Seacombe to New Brighton and it was a busy and bustling thoroughfare.

Victoria Road, Seacombe, just by the ferry, in 1908. This is now Victoria Place and has changed completely. 'Entwistle Brothers Quality Teeth' are being advertised under the clock tower on the right.

One of the great delights of a holiday or day out on the Wallasey side of Wirral was a chance to take a stroll along the wide promenade and watch the activities of the ships on the River Mersey. Here we see a full promenade at Seacombe, *c.* 1904. The ships in mid-river are at anchor, not sailing. Companies did this sometimes out of necessity because the Pier Head was full or the docks were full, and sometimes they anchored-out to save money. It was much cheaper to anchor-out – no tying-up charges, no dockers' wages to pay, etc. The company would also retain much more control of their ships – the staff for instance could not slip up or down the gangway but could instead be 'logged' on and off the ship. Sometimes ships would just come alongside for an hour or so before they sailed but many just sailed from anchor, meaning they could sail at any time but the lowest of tides. From the docks, you would have to wait until high tide. In the background you can see the four funnels of the *Mauretania*.

Seacombe ferry terminus on a quiet afternoon, *c.* 1910. This terminus never had the same bustle as Birkenhead. It lacked a railway station and choice of tram routes. Nevertheless, in another two hours the workers will be flooding home and then day trippers returning to Liverpool will fill the area, but just for now things seem very quiet.

A Wallasey bus outside the Seacombe ferry terminal, *c.* 1960. It had a sea-green and cream livery. Note the Wallasey coat of arms in stone on the terminal behind the bus. This Leyland bus, bought new in July 1955, was later sold to the Castrol Oil Company and spent many years taking their workers to Stanlow Refinery at Ellesmere Port.

Wallasey bus no. 45 on the 17 service from Seacombe to New Brighton via Poulton Road, *c.* 1960. Pictured in Poulton Road, it looks to have only a few passengers. Bought in February 1951, the bus (AHF 841) was sold in April 1970.

New Brighton

The New Brighton I remember – the fairground in 1962. New Brighton was the dream of two Liverpool men, James Atherton and Mr Agnew, who bought land on the north-east corner of Wirral and planned to develop a holiday resort. At the end of the nineteenth century they laid out the town and their plans to emulate not the Brighton down south but Blackpool. The sands were there, the pier and ferry services were there, and the people were there, in Liverpool just across the Mersey. It could not fail. It didn't, then it did, then it didn't, then it did. That was the story of New Brighton, all ups and downs. Success then struggle. New Brighton has always had to compete with more established resorts. It never seemed to have the tone or class of Brighton in the south, or the business and brashness of Lancashire's Blackpool, but it was not for want of trying. (*Len Jackson*)

The New Brighton
pier as it appeared
up to 1867, which
makes this a very early
photograph. In 1863
Coulbourn & Co., who
owned New Brighton
Ferry, sold the rights
to Wallasey Local
Government Board who
're-built the wooden
pier with a floating
iron one', which
opened in 1867. This
must therefore be the
original pier and our
postcard must be from
the 1950s.

New Brighton was a popular place in the years after the Second World War. True, the tower had gone, but the tower ballroom and fairground made up for that and the shows and children's entertainment were second-to-none. You could get there in an hour from anywhere in Liverpool. That was if you were not caught up in the queue to get on or off the ferry. Our 1949 photograph shows just how crowded the pier could be with the passengers disembarking.

A Bank Holiday Crowd at New Brighton.

An Edwardian photograph taken from the end of the pier looking up Victoria Street. The crowds speak for themselves and reflect the glory of New Brighton's past. The buildings on the right were known as the 'ham & egg parade' and would serve breakfast for early visitors. I was once told that full breakfast was one price (say 2/-) before 8.00 a.m. and then 6*d* dearer from 8 to 9 a.m. From 10 to 11 a.m. there was a final chance for ham & eggs but at 3/6*d*. It is a great anecdote and it is told by quite a few older people who would have been around in the 1920s, but I have never been able to verify it.

Same time, same place as the picture above but looking the other way. We are in the late Edwardian period and the pier has a Victorian solidness and grandeur about it. The 'S' code on the tram was for Seacombe and the 'WD' was for Wallasey Docks.

The pier, New Brighton, from a 1930s postcard. This shows clearly that there were in fact two piers at New Brighton: one for 'promenading' (the left-hand one) and one for getting on and off the ferries. Wallasey Corporation owned New Brighton pier from *c.* 1864 and ran it for over a century. The second pier seen here was built in 1921. The problem with New Brighton pier was that, being at the mouth of the river, silt gathered in any deep parts. The more the ferry company dredged to keep the water deep around the pier, the more silt and mud was attracted.

The promenade and Battery at New Brighton, *c.* 1904. The Rock Battery was completed in about 1825, supposedly to defend the River Mersey. But it is said that the cannons were only ever fired twice, and then by mistake. Over the years the Battery has had a few different uses, and at one time gunpowder from visiting vessels would be stored there for safety while the ship was in port. In the 1950s and 1960s it became an amusement centre and, as you could only get there at low and mid-tide, it was quite exciting to visit, and added to the thrill of the day. Today it is a museum, much more fitting, and well worth a visit.

Wirral was blessed with three large open-air swimming pools (known as lidos). The biggest and grandest of them was the one at New Brighton, opened by Lord Leverhulme in June 1934. Above we see it in 1937 when hundreds of youngsters took part in a Coronation physical culture display in the drained pool. This massive open-air pool was popular with all the family because it had one sloping side and went from nothing to 12ft. Toddlers could paddle in safety and for a time it even had a 'sand beach' in one area for the young ones to play on.

New Brighton open-air bathing pool, pictured here during a heat from the 'Miss New Brighton' contest from around the late 1950s. The contest was one of the most popular parts of the holiday, held every Wednesday throughout the season with the final at the end of August drawing massive crowds. One advertisement I have seen says 'It's the ideal start for Models and Starlets'. Girls went to New Brighton on holiday and entered the competition with high hopes. If you won a heat the Corporation made sure that your home town local paper carried a photograph of your success.

An aerial view of New Brighton, *c.* 1920. The tower is in the process of being demolished owing to neglect and lack of maintenance. You can see Perch Rock and the pier but the foreground is dominated by New Brighton's cemetery.

The tower at New Brighton was modelled on the Eiffel Tower in Paris. Gustave Eiffel's creation had caused a fever, caught first by Blackpool, then Wembley and New Brighton. Here we see the tower at New Brighton, at the peak of its popularity. It was 621ft high (higher than Blackpool Tower) and was completed and opened in 1898. It was declared unsafe in 1919 and its owners were told to spend money on it or pull it down. When the summer season started in 1922 there was no sign of our famous landmark, just the tower buildings below.

The car and coach park next to New Brighton's open-air swimming pool, *c.* 1946. This photograph came out of a file on parking difficulties at this site. Study it closely and you'll see some of the cars still have white bumpers, painted on for wartime. On the skyline can be seen the funnels of Cunard, B & I and CP ships so I would estimate the date to be just after the Second World War. Our picture proves how popular New Brighton was, especially with the Cheshire towns and the industrial towns of South Lancashire. It really was a rival, and a strong one at that, to Blackpool and Southport in the late 1940s and 1950s. As a child from Widnes I went to Blackpool once in about 1956 but was taken to New Brighton at least ten times. Collectors and restorers of vintage coaches will like this picture with its Leylands, Daimlers, Ribbles, etc. – they are all there.

This is the New Brighton I remember. This is the pleasure resort of my childhood, nearly half a century ago. Taken from the top of the tower buildings, *c.* 1959, it shows the big dipper, helter skelter and big wheel which all gave so much amusement and thrills to the 1950s teenager. 'Baby boom', 'Teddy Boys', 'Mods' and 'Rockers', 'Flappers' and 'Gay Young Things' – New Brighton has seen the lot and coped! Looking at the water you realise why New Brighton had so many problems with silting around the pier. After the Second World War the ferry company gave up the fight with the river during the winter and just ran summer services. Dredging would start two weeks before Easter. Just for the record *Empress of England* is in the dock on the far side of the river. (*Len Jackson*)

The beach at New Brighton, *c.* 1959, and what a busy scene we have. The tower buildings brought a lot of business to the town. Bob Wooler and NEMS (Brian Epstein) both promoted dances there because it could hold thousands, had a decent smallish stage, a reasonable sound system, and was cheap to hire. What more could you ask for? I wrote for a magazine called *Mersey Beat* at the time and ran coach parties from Widnes to the tower. I have sat in that dressing room with Little Richard, Jerry Lee Lewis, the Rolling Stones, the Beatles, and many, many more. The tower buildings burnt down in April 1969 and the 'swinging sixties' came to an abrupt end for New Brighton.

The tower buildings dominating another view over New Brighton beach. This time it is early morning, before breakfast in the summer of 1963 (I am told) but it could have been anytime in the 1960s. The Tivoli Theatre on the right had been a Mecca entertainment of all types for many years. It opened at Easter in 1914 and Lillie Langtry topped the bill. It had a large café running right along the front, on the first floor, and six shops at the front. Close inspection of this photograph shows the shops boarded up. The Tivoli closed as a theatre in April 1955 then spent some years as an arcade and a café. There was a fire in 1976 after which the building was pulled down. The water is a children's paddling and boating pool created by a small concrete wall that traps the water as the tide goes out.

Royal Iris was the 'Queen' of the river in the 1950s and 1960s. There were 'Jazz Cruises', 'Rock Cruises', 'Afternoon Tea Dances' etc., and always lots going on. Wallasey Corporation even re-modelled one of their buses to look like the ship. This is what we see here, doubler-decker Leyland 'Titan' no. 27 (bought in 1948), which had been converted in February 1960 and ran right through that decade for publicity. It is seen here on the New Brighton Marine Parade near Rowson Street.

New Brighton was a place of family fun, a place where the teenagers of the 'swinging sixties' could stretch their wings and meet people. Here we have a typical publicity photograph from the Corporation showing three happy teenagers being doused with water by the pool attendant (complete with quiff and DA) – all good innocent fun, out in the fresh air. Of course foreign holidays put an end to these out-door swimming pools, people now prefer warmer climes before divesting themselves of their clothes. Part of the Derby Pool at the end of Kings Parade, New Brighton, is still there; it is now a theme pub and restaurant and is still a very pleasant place to visit.

George Felton was the 'Donkey Man' on New Brighton beach right through the 1950s. He is seen here with three young charges setting out for an adventure. Once the tower had burnt down, the funfair closed and the pier was dismantled, New Brighton again went into decline.

Beside the Seaside

A composite card from Moreton – 'the poor man's New Brighton'. Once a place becomes popular, it becomes crowded, then you get two classes of people who look for somewhere else. Some want either a quieter or a cheaper holiday while others (usually works managers or shop foremen) want to go somewhere different, away from the working classes. This happened on the Lancashire coast, where Southport and Lytham St Annes came to be considered as classier than Blackpool. On Wirral, Hoylake and West Kirby were considered to be far superior places to New Brighton, Moreton and Liscard which were much cheaper. Because Wallasey had 7 miles of beach and the urban district of Hoylake another 8, there was plenty of choice. New Brighton's popularity turned off just as many people as it turned on.

Wallasey Corporation undertook to build sea defences along the top edge of Wirral (the embankment). There was an embankment committee and the situation was reviewed with the Mersey Docks & Harbour Board regularly. From New Brighton to Moreton, the embankment was known as 'Mock Beggar's Wharf' after a hall which stood in the area.

Moreton was a fishing and farming community which took in visitors when New Brighton was full. Moreton in the pre-war years was the destination of many church outings. The Farmer's Arms at Moreton is seen on our postcard of about 1906. Walking, fresh air, seeing the old village – pleasures that many today have lost the knack of enjoying – were all most people wanted from a holiday in those days.

The charms of rural Moreton, combined with the beach and sand, have, over the years, provided thousands with a cheap and peaceful holiday. Mary Anne's Lane, says the caption on this card, and I wonder if she is the lady with the white apron. This view is from around 1910.

Hoylake Road, Moreton, *c.* 1930. Ever since people started travelling for pleasure Wirral has been a great place for a trip. There is a lot to see in such a small area. Moreton is still a favourite day out for many people from Liverpool.

Moreton Cross and its unusual-shaped roundabout, seen here in 1955. Moreton was home to a very famous jockey called Gem Mason who won the Grand National a few times. Every time he won he put his money away and he built those shops on the far side (right) with the winnings. The fronts of the shops carried the names of his great winning rides.

In the years between the wars, a whole tent city would be pitched on the Moreton/ Leasowe border in the summer. These tents provided cheap breaks for families who would not have had a holiday otherwise. Our photograph captures one of those happy families – with nine children and five adults, I wonder if they were all staying in 'The Mush'.

A composite card of Leasowe, *c.* 1925. Leasowe Castle was the main feature of the area. The name was given to a castellated hall, said to have been built by Lord Derby in the reign of Elizabeth I. It had previously been called Mock Beggar Hall, and was built half-way between the Mersey and the Dee, so that both rivers could be watched from the hall's roof. When it was sold and converted into a luxury hotel it was renamed 'Leasowe Castle'. Early in the 1900s it became a convalescent home for the railway union, then it went back to being an hotel in the 1970s. The fittings from the famous Star Chamber in Westminster were said to have been given to Lord Derby and fitted here.

West Kirby promenade, with visitors and locals enjoying a stroll and the sea air. This card was posted in 1916 during the First World War but not many new cards came out in war time and the hats definitely look Edwardian so this picture probably dates to about 1912. The houses on the left took in boarders or lodgers in the season and let out spare rooms.

Meols (pronounced Mells) Drive, West Kirby, in the early 1920s. I have always wondered about the coast road from New Brighton to West Kirby. There are no obstacles so one would expect a long straight road, developed from a walking path or cart track. Instead the road swings inland from the coast, with numerous tight bends and the like.

West Kirby shore and the beach, c. 1920. There are only four houses in our picture. Soon after this, the building boom started here and now there are no empty spaces at all along the front. Note the horse-drawn wagon on the beach.

Hoylake's open-air bathing pool, seen here in the mid-1950s. What a grand pool it was! Hoylake as a holiday resort was created by Sir John Stanley, who in 1792 built the Royal Hotel here. The Stanley family loved horse racing and encouraged it at their Knowsley Estate in Liverpool, and in 1847 horse racing moved here as well. The Royal Liverpool Hunt Cup was held here until 1868. The hotel was demolished, but the area had been laid out by Sir John and it developed into a resort just as he planned.

Another view of the bathing pool at Hoylake, 1938. This view is looking up the promenade towards Wallasey and includes some of the front. The name Hoylake comes from Hoyle Lake, 'The lake in the hollow'. The lake in question is thought to have been in the Queen's Park area.

Market Street in the very centre of Hoylake in 1907. It is a very rural scene with horse-drawn carts delivering goods to the shops. One of Hoylake's claims to fame is that in 1689 William of Orange and his supporters sailed from here to Ireland to defeat James II and secure the throne for William. The King's Gap off Market Street is said to mark the way William went to his ship and the road is still known by that name today.

Market Street leads to Birkenhead Road, shown in this photograph at the very start of the 1900s. Until about two hundred years ago this area was just a fishing village with some farms on the outskirts. Then a number of Liverpool shipping barons came here to build summer villas for themselves away from the grimy Liverpool air. Because of its situation Hoylake has long been an important lifeboat station. The first lifeboat here was recorded in 1803 when a boat from Liverpool was brought to Hoylake where it was housed in a wooden boat house built for it by the Mersey Docks & Harbour Board.

'Having a lovely time. Wish you were here.' Fun on the sands of Hoylake in the 1920s. J.T. Clarke is the name on the side of the donkeys' feeding box. If you got bored with the sands there was, and still is, a lovely walk to the Red Rocks. If you are careful and take note of the tide times you can walk out past Little and Middle Eye and end up on Hilbre Island. But if you miss the tide you could be stuck there for up to eight hours. Hilbre has been a monastery, a retreat and a lifeboat station, and there is even evidence of Bronze Age occupation. It is now a bird sanctuary, established in 1957.

A postcard from Valentine's of Dundee, showing Market Street, Hoylake, in the mid-1960s. The zebra crossing leads to Hoylake Urban District Council's town hall on the right of the picture. Like those of Wallasey and Birkenhead, Hoylake UDC was absorbed into the Metropolitan Borough of Wirral in April 1974.

Parkgate, Wirral, caught at a rare moment when the tide was high and even breaking over on to the road. Our photograph is from around 1930, but Parkgate goes back a lot further in time than that. There has been a harbour here since Tudor times and, as the River Dee silted up, it became increasingly busy as first Chester then Neston lost their ability to handle the sailing ships from Ireland. In the late 1600s most ships sailed from Parkgate and it was an important port until the early nineteenth century when it became too shallow for the ships.

During the years when Parkgate was a port it acquired all the buildings needed to function as such – an hotel, harbour master's house and of course a customs house. All of these are still there today and add to the charm of the place. Here we see the Watch House as it was in the 1920s. Note that there is quite a slope down to the river where two rowing boats are ready for use on the slip-way.

'A Sunday Afternoon' says our 1957 postcard of Parkgate. You can see that the mud and silt has grass growing on it. Today the silt is almost level with the footpath and water just creeps in two or three times a year at very high tide with the wind blowing in from the Irish Sea. You can see the Ship Hotel on the right and Parkgate's famous ice cream shop next door and can you make out the wrought iron balcony of the Customs House further up?

A clever postcard from the 1960s. In 1960 Parkgate was still a fishing port and there was still a cut-out to the Dee but the battle against the silt was soon lost and fishing from here was abandoned. The composer Handel once stayed here while waiting to sail to Dublin. He did some of the work on his *Messiah* while staying at an hotel in Parkgate.

Rural Wirral

The windmill on Bidston Hill, a conservation victory in recent years, and seen here in a picture from 1946.

No one who has lived or worked on Wirral over the last fifty years can fail to appreciate the quieter, rural side of this peninsula. Nearly everybody wants to live in or next to a quaint little village, yet these villages are themselves having to fight off extra housing developments which threaten their very character. Village shops are struggling for existence as people now shop at the larger supermarkets for convenience and cheapness. Of Wirral's 60 square miles over 40 are still green areas and need to stay that way.

The villages of Wirral are unbelievably charming and many still retain features from a century or more ago. I can see a problem in years to come when pleasure motoring and driving round the villages will become so popular that places will clog up and we will have residents-only parking and one-way systems through the narrow streets. Now that ordering water or orange juice in a pub or restaurant has become more socially acceptable people can 'drink and drive', and this has brought a revival for the rural inns of Wirral. There are some great old inns serving good food and it is quite an adventure to try to winkle them out.

Caldy village, 1917. Caldy or 'Cold-ey' means 'the cold area that floods and makes an island' and the name comes from Scandinavia.

The Wheatsheaf Inn in the village of Raby, Wirral. This hostelry has provided refreshment for travellers for around four hundred years. Raby today is still one of the quieter and more cut-off villages. The name Raby also comes from Scandinavia and means 'the village near the boundary mark', though exactly where the Norse boundary was we are not sure.

Eastham, though included in our ferry section, has a large village inland from the river bank. Here we see the village centre and church which contains the tombs of the Hooton branch of the Stanley family.

A view of Eastham village from the very start of the 1900s. The Hooton Arms on the far side of the road has now gone. The building nearest the camera on the left is the village post office and even has a clock on the wall outside.

There were gardens and entertainment pavilions all over Wirral. Here we see the Fred Brooks' Vaudeville Troupe who played Eastham Gardens for the summer of 1909. There was always some sort of outdoor entertainment in all the leisure gardens, and it must have kept acts such as these in full employment for many years.

The old windmill at Willaston, shown in a rather sorry state, *c.* 1930. Built in 1800 to replace an old 'Peg Mill', it was the largest of the Old Wirral flour mills. The one thing Wirral lacked was water power – it had no fast-flowing river and so people turned to wind power. There were probably as many as forty windmills on Wirral by 1700, but only seven water mills. The mill in this picture was purchased by the Wirral branch of the council as part of the preservation of rural England scheme in May 1936, and a lot of work has since gone into halting its deterioration.

'The post office, Woodchurch', *c.* 1908, in the then village of Woodchurch. It is keeping its purpose a closely guarded secret and the ivy-covered cottage has none of the hype and bustle usually associated with local post offices. The wooden church which gave Woodchurch its name was rebuilt in the thirteenth century and its square tower is incorporated into the church today. It is famous for a Saxon cross and its stained-glass and decoration.

Heswall was the old capital of Wirral. Long before Birkenhead started to expand, Heswall had a court and meeting place. The name means 'hazel trees by a stream'. Although it has lost a lot of its civic importance, Heswall still has a prosperous air about it and has lost none of its civic pride. This 1910 postcard captures the Rocky Lane area, a small corner of the village.

The village blacksmith at Burton, Wirral, attending to a lady with a horse and gig at the end of the nineteenth century. Burton is one of the more isolated of Wirral's villages. The lady could be from Burton Manor nearby, the Congreve family home. General Walter Congreve won a VC at Colenso, and his son Walter La Touche Congreve also won a VC in France in 1916. Only three fathers and sons have ever done this. The village has two important religious connections. It is the birth- place of Thomas Wilson, one time Bishop of Sodor and Man, who spent his whole life in helpful service to his fellow man. His only boast was that he was 'the poorest Bishop in Europe.' It is also the last resting place of the Blessed Father Plessington, executed at Chester in 1679 for being a priest.

The Clegg Inn at Heswall, Cheshire. It would be hard to date this picture except for the small sign near the gentleman on the right which proclaims that 'Ford motor cars can be serviced here at a branch of Blake & Co. of Rodney Street, Liverpool.' That puts it at around 1910. The inn is still there today but has been changed and added to over the years.

Main Street, now Chester Road, at Bromborough, *c.* 1905. The road that people rush down today at Bromborough is not the original Chester Road. This is what is now called Bromborough village, looking back towards Birkenhead from the southern end of that stretch of highway. Bromborough had three wells at one time – the name means 'place of wells or springs' – St Chad's Well, St Patrick's Well and the old Petrifying Well.

A very early postcard showing the centre of Old Bebington village a century ago. The combined signpost, drinking fountain and gas light is quite unusual. 'Ascroft's' was a newsagents on one side and fruiterers on the other, and looks like the only shop open on that row. Bebington was incorporated as a municipal borough in 1937. The village was first mentioned in 1090 when Hugh de Boydell issued a charter confirming that the area belonged to one Robert de Lancelyn.

A charming scene at the anniversary celebrations of the church at Higher Bebington. Prior to passing the Local Government Act of 1894, Higher and Lower Bebington were separate entities from Bebington itself. Called Bebington Superior at one time, its church is not one of the ancient ones of Wirral so the anniversary is probably only for fifty or sixty years. The church does have some beautiful Burne-Jones windows.

A quiet, reflective moment down in Bromborough Woods. It is near here that the lime-rich water of the petrifying spring flows into an old stone basin. The bridge that our young gent is sitting on is over the small River Dibben. On old maps the wood is marked as St Patrick's Wood.

Now just an outlying part of Birkenhead, Upton was once a separate village. It enjoyed a fine position on higher ground and gave views over to the Irish Sea. This Edwardian photograph, of about 1908, has the added interest of the boys playing on the quiet road; three of them have iron hoops.

Irby village, *c.* 1904. The thatched cottage on the right was the village post office. Outside we can see two fine examples of very early children's pushchairs or prams. Irby is one of the ancient Scandinavian names which abound on Wirral. It means 'the place where the Irishmen live', but probably refers to Vikings who had moved there from Ireland.

Bedford Road, Rock Ferry, looking down from the railway station in the early years of the 1900s. Bedford Road led from the railway station (Rock Ferry) down to the pier and was a very busy road. Visitors would be advised to cross from Liverpool by Underground then make their way down Bedford Road and take the ferry back. There was a cab stand on the left of the picture and maybe the sailors and the youngsters are waiting for a cab to take them down to the ferry. What a pleasant and interesting round trip.

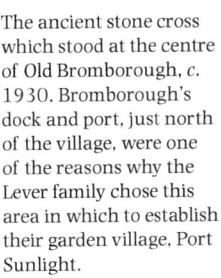

The ancient stone cross which stood at the centre of Old Bromborough, c. 1930. Bromborough's dock and port, just north of the village, were one of the reasons why the Lever family chose this area in which to establish their garden village, Port Sunlight.

A social occasion has always been something to look forward to and Cheshire villages seem to throw themselves into these events with more gusto than most. Wirral does not let Cheshire down. Here is the Ladies' Club, Neston, going to church in 1907. There's a policeman at the front, and one or two 'dons' complete with cap and gown, and several gentlemen in top hats (and the odd bowler). It looks to be an important event, as everyone is dressed in their Sunday best.

The High Street, Neston, caught on camera a century ago. One of Neston's claims to fame is that Lady Hamilton, 'friend' of Lord Nelson, was born here as Emma Lyon in about 1761. They had a daughter who married a vicar and bore him eight children. Neston also has many literary connections. Anna Seward wrote a book here called *A Nest from the Storm of the Ocean*. Charles Kingsley told a pathetic tale of 'Mary', trapped by the creeping tide as she drove cattle across the sands at Neston, and local man Samuel Warren wrote the Victorian best-seller *Ten Thousand A Year* at the Quay House here.

A ploughing match
in progress on Wirral
in 1932. What an
evocative picture of a
bygone era.

The blacksmith and
his assistant hard
at work inside the
village smithy at Little
Stanney, Wirral, in
1932.

The village of Burton, Wirral, in 1934. (*Liverpool Daily Post & Echo*)

The windmill on Bidston Hill, Wirral, photographed in 1933.

Sport and Relaxation

An amateur golf match in progress at the Royal Course at Hoylake in August 1933. The cameraman noticed that a storm over Wales was giving the sky a strange dark look as he took this picture for the *Liverpool Daily Post & Echo*.

'The Leisure Peninsula' was one description of Wirral in the mid-1960s. It really was a place where people could enjoy many sports and pastimes. The fact that there was so much open space helped, but someone had to provide the facilities and there had to be enough people to use them. Even today, many people flock to Wirral to walk, sail, play golf, ride their bikes and enjoy both the country and sea air.

One of Wirral's gems is the Royal Liverpool Golf Course at Hoylake. It is said to be the finest in the area and one of the best in the country. There were once three magnificent open-air swimming pools on Wirral, which were very popular not only with swimmers but with canoeists too. In fact, as the slogan said, Wirral was the place for sport and relaxation.

Long gone are the days when Tranmere Rovers were the joke team of Merseyside. As the year 2000 season starts they are in the First Division. Here we see them on 13 November 1950 during a game against Chester. Payne, Rovers' goal-keeper, punches the ball away from Hankinson, Burgess and Devonshire from Chester as no. 6 Keiran and no. 3 Hodgson look on. (*Liverpool Daily Post & Echo*)

Birkenhead Park was always one of the leading rugby union teams in the north of England. Its members resisted the change to rugby league a century ago, and carry on the 'Gentleman's Game' today. Here we see them in March 1921 playing Hull and East Riding. Birkenhead star Lowry 'the speed merchant' has the ball. 'Old Birkenians' were another of the leading rugby union teams of the area.

Action at the Wirral
Harriers point-to-point at
Ledsham in spring 1934.
Horse riding, point-to-
point and the Wirral hunt
have always been big on
the calendar here. Do not
forget there was once a
laid-out racecourse where
the Royal Liverpool Club
House is today. It was
created by one of the
Stanley family and the
road which leads there
is called Stanley Road.
(*Liverpool Daily Post &
Echo*)

Golf was first recorded on Wirral in 1852 when a few Scottish settlers at West Kirby decided to relieve their
homesickness by playing a round of golf on a nearby rabbit warren. In 1869 a club was formed, and in
1871 HRH the Duke of Connaught became President, and it was renamed the Royal Liverpool Golf Club. This
postcard from 1907 shows a match-day at the club. I have looked very closely but can only spot one lady on
this picture and she is in the left-hand corner.

West Kirby in the 1930s. Wirral prided itself on giving visitors plenty to keep them occupied. Cricket matches were organised and there were plenty of bowling greens.

Birkenhead says farewell to the Wirral's greatest sporting hero. William Ralph Dean played his first game for Tranmere Rovers in January 1924 and on 21 March 1925 played his first game for Everton. He once scored all five goals when Manchester United were beaten 5–2 at Everton and held the club record of sixty goals in one season. He played 43 times for Everton, scored 377 goals and won 16 caps for England. He died in 1980, just minutes before the end of a match at Goodison. Here we see some of the thousands who turned up at the church in Birkenhead to give the great man a 'crowd' for his send-off. (*Liverpool Daily Post & Echo*)

Port Sunlight

Poets Corner, Port Sunlight, showing off its quiet charm in 1909. Port Sunlight is the dream of William Hesketh Lever. He was one of the few industrialists in history who meant every word he said, who led by example and who really did have the interest of his works close to his heart.

A Lancashire lad from Bolton, he started a firm called Lever Bros to make purer soap. The first factory was in Warrington in 1886 but the success of his product meant that he needed to expand. William Lever was very forward-thinking, and knew that the ship canal would bring changes to the River Mersey and cause problems for his distribution system. In 1888, after looking round for the most suitable spot, he found Bromborough pool, and decided that this was where he would build his dream. Port Sunlight is not just the houses and village on the left of New Chester Road – it is also the docks, the seed crushing plant, the printing works, court house and cricket ground as well.

Lever believed that nothing was ugly, that there was beauty in everything if it was brought out well. In 1889 he expounded his humanitarian feelings and said that unless things changed every field would be a factory, every street a slum, and lowly workers would be slaves. He led the way in showing that the cheapest way was not always the best. He pushed and planned until the marshy creek was a dock able to take ocean-going ships to and from all corners of the globe. He put into his plans for the village two schools, a hospital, a swimming pool, a social club and a village hall, making it a veritable paradise for his workers.

Bolton Road runs right through the centre of Port Sunlight and was named to remind William Lever of his roots. He commissioned thirty different architects to work on Port Sunlight so that there would be a diversity of style and ideas in the village. It is said that there are over seven hundred houses and no two blocks are the same. He laid down the best sanitation, the widest roads, and planted trees everywhere. Even in the school he demanded teachers with a joy of imparting knowledge, and a love for their vocation.

This is one of the show houses of the estate, a house modelled on the very place where England's greatest writer was born. A leaflet from 1910 proudly states that after five years' service workers over the age of twenty-five received shares in the company. Ladies worked four hours less a week than the men and when asked to work overtime were given a tea-break and provided with tea at the company's expense. Not long after this they included travel tokens for all those who did not live in the village, as the council of Lower Bebington had refused to let the Birkenhead Corporation lay tram lines out to Port Sunlight and refused planning permission for a private railway platform so workers could catch the train right to Port Sunlight works. William Lever laid on his own transport system to get round the very obstinate council.

Some of the social amenities that were laid on are shown here in our 1935 Frith postcard. The Heritage Centre occupies this site today and they have plans and scale models of the origins of Port Sunlight. Today, the village is run by the Port Sunlight Trust, although many of the houses have been sold off recently. The whole village is a conservation area and it is a pleasure to visit. Everywhere gardens bloom, and are neat and colourful even in winter. You need a pride in your home and a sense of community spirit to live in Port Sunlight – ideals the founder would have applauded.

When William Lever's wife, his lifelong supporter and friend, died, he built in her memory the wonderful Lady Lever Art Gallery. When William Lever died in 1925, the people of Port Sunlight built a monument to his memory, with five figures that represent his lifelong ideals – Inspiration, Industry, Education, Charity and Art. The greatest tribute to him is that what he put in place, and the trust he laid for the future, is still there and working today. His great personal gift was the church at Port Sunlight, Christ Church, and it is there that William and his wife lie in peace. As I write in July 2000 the death has just been announced of the 3rd Lord Leverhulme, grandson of William Lever. I wonder if he will go to his rest with his illustrious ancestor?

Workers at Ellesmere Port demonstrate their support for the Cheshire Regiment at the start of the First World War. The borough of Ellesmere Port got its Charter of Incorporation on 29 March 1955 and on 7 May 1955 HRH the Duchess of Kent presented the town with its charter. Ellesmere Port Borough covered 9,144 acres, with a population of just under 40,000 people. Overpool, Netherpool, Little Sutton and Sutton were part of that borough.

Ellesmere Port was called Whitby two centuries ago, and before that it was looked on as the land of Stanlow Abbey, a Cistercian monastery. Here we see barges coming into the port in an atmospheric photograph from 1929. (*Liverpool Daily Post & Echo*)

Wirral Today

The Lady Lever Art Gallery, Port Sunlight, a chance for everyone to enjoy the great paintings of the pre-Raphaelites Rossetti and Ford Maddox Brown.

On 1 April 1974 the county borough of Birkenhead and Wallasey came together. Joining them that day was the Borough of Bebington and the UDCs of Hoylake and Wirral. These all made up the Metropolitan Borough of Wirral, with an estimated population, at that time, of 333,700.

Wirral has a long and proud tradition and will build on that for a prosperous future. The coat of arms and motto adopted is 'By Faith and Foresight'. The symbols of Birkenhead and Wirral are the oyster catcher and bog myrtle, which stand for the wild life and nature side of our peninsula, while the green shield and horn reflect the rural aspect. On either side of the shield are blue and white waves, representing the Dee and Mersey which lie on either side of the peninsula.

Wirral seems to be coming out of the shadow of its cross-river neighbour. Over the past few years Birkenhead Docks has been home for balloon festivals, river fireworks and other events. The Wirral Show is more popular than ever, and tourism is on the up-and-up.

The heritage tram at the Woodside ferry terminal is a refurbished one from 1880 when George Train introduced Britain's first tram to Birkenhead. Outside the terminal during the summer you can see a full-size replica of an electric tram from 1902. Just down the road at Shore Road pumping station you can see a restored 80ft Grasshopper steam beam engine working when the trams are running. Not far away are the historic warships and the awesome outline of a U-boat, perhaps the most feared fighting machine of the Second World War. It is made all the more chilling because this is the only U-boat to have been raised from the sea-bed.

The Mersey may have less bustle and fewer ships than yesteryear but we still get some excitement when the river entertains visitors. Here, framed next to the last One O'Clock Gun is the aircraft carrier *Invincible*, on a Royal Navy visit in July 2000. The *QEII* has been a regular visitor, and the Mersey River Festival draws large numbers of visitors and exhibitors each year.

The ferry company (or, to give it its full title, the Mersey Passenger Transport Executive) is working hard on Merseyside transport on both sides of the river. For every person who gets on the ferry at the weekend for a Heritage Cruise and to learn about the history of the ferries, another passenger gets on just to cross the river quickly, and another will get on to relive the days of youth and enjoy a trip to New Brighton or a Beat Cruise with the Beatles or Swinging Blue Jeans. The ferries are different things to different people.

At Seacombe Ferry in 1991 an aquarium opened that transformed the ferry terminal. It is a great teaching aid as well as fun to visit, and there is a 'hands on' area for youngsters. Here we see Ollie the Octopus. The trips from Liverpool up the ship canal to Manchester are proving more popular each year. You do see a whole new side to the areas of Ellesmere Port, Warrington and Runcorn as the ship passes through. It would be nice if one of the ferry services could recreate the days out to Llandudno and Beaumaris that so delighted our parents and grandparents.

This is the redundant Mersey tunnel entrance in the Four Bridges area of Birkenhead. It is sad to see it in such a neglected state – maybe it could be turned into a 'time tunnel' going back to the Bronze Age. Even a wine bar or theme pub would be better than nothing – at least you would be able to park.

This is me – I like to get my face in each of my books – to upset the historians in the future! I read so many old books and wonder what the authors were like. If you listen to Radio Merseyside long enough I am bound to pop up somewhere. But at least we have met, even if we haven't been formally introduced.

Acknowledgements

Thanks are due to Reg Wilson of West Kirby; to Jack Barlow for his help and advice with the bus photographs; to David Roberts for permission to use his Cammell Laird photographs, especially the Polaris ones; and to Gordon Coltas (Locofotos) for the great photographic record he has of Birkenhead Woodside railway station.

Special thanks must go to Andrew Almond and Wendy of A & A Publicity for making available their old Wirral photographs. They hold the archive of Living Memories and gave me access to it. To Ted Gerry of New Brighton, one of the gentlemen of the postcard collectors, for his help in finding some of the rarer village postcards. Thanks to Colin Hunt from the library of the *Liverpool Daily Post & Echo*, always a patient helper, who released some of the *Post*'s rarer pictures for use. To Michael Day for permission to reproduce his photographs. To my good friend Ged McCann for his photographs of Birkenhead today and his help in saving some of the older prints. To F. Leonard (Len) Jackson for permission to include some of the great photographs he took in the early and middle part of the century. To Alan B. Cross for permission to include his bus photographs and to Mr R.H.G. Simpson for his transport photographs.

Sunset over Birkenhead on 1 January 2000, the first sunset of a new century. What will that new century hold? How will we record 2001, 2100 and the future? It's up to you!